Shropshire Seasons

Gordon Dickins

Shropshire
Books

Front cover: River Teme, Bromfield.

Back cover: Berrington

© Gordon Dickins 1993

ISBN: 0-903802-58-9

Cover and book design: Paul Brasenell

Editing: Helen Sample

Published by Shropshire Books,
the Publishing Division of the Leisure Services Department
of Shropshire County Council.

Printed by Precision Colour Printing, Telford.

Shropshire Seasons

*F*or *J*ulie

Acknowledgements

I am most grateful for the interest, support and help given to me in the preparation of this book by many friends and colleagues. In particular I should like to thank the following:

J ohn Hirst for inviting me to produce the book in the first place; Bob Kemp and John Reader for providing a selection of superb natural history photographs to supplement my own scenic shots; Helen Sample who has not only edited the book but offered continued encouragement and enthusiasm for the project; Paul Brasenell for his excellent design. Finally, and as always, my thanks to Julie for putting up with yet another of my photographic obsessions.

T echnical Details: Most of my photographs were taken with a Nikon FM2 camera and Sigma 28-70 and 70-210 mm lenses on, for the most part, Agfa or Fuji slide film.

T he publishers wish to thank the following for providing the natural history photographs reproduced in this book: Bob Kemp pp. 1, 6 (primroses), 7, 35, 47, 109, 128; John Reader pp. 6 (cowslip), 77, 87, 108, 113, 146; the remaining photographs are by Gordon Dickins.

T he publishers would also like to thank Elizabeth Jennings for her kind permission to reproduce her poem "Song at the Begining of Autumn" on pp. 77, and the copyright holders (or their representatives) for extracts from the following works:- "A Shropshire Lad", A. E. Housman; "Sowing", Edward Thomas; "Precious Bane", Mary Webb; "Viroconium", Mary Webb; "Tess of the D'Urbervilles", Thomas Hardy; "A Shot Magpie", Andrew Young; "Neutral Tones", Thomas Hardy; "The Golden Arrow", Mary Webb; "St. Mawr", D. H. Lawrence.

About the Author

*G*ordon Dickins was brought up in the Shropshire village of Coalport and attended schools in Coalbrookdale and Madeley before taking a degree in English at the University College of North Wales, Bangor. He then worked as a library assistant with Shropshire County Library and went on to complete a post-graduate course in librarianship at Manchester Polytechnic. Returning to Shropshire he worked in libraries in Shrewsbury, Market Drayton and Wellington. Since 1980 he has specialised in children's librarianship and is currently head of Children's and Schools' Library Services within Shropshire County Council's Leisure Services Department.

*G*ordon has been involved in photography for fifteen years, the Shropshire landscape being his favourite subject, and has had photographs published in magazines and local publications. A parallel interest is the literary history of the county and he is the author of *An Illustrated Literary Guide to Shropshire* and co-author of *Walks with Writers*. He has contributed to Radio Shropshire and Radio 4 programmes on Shropshire writers and to the Channel 4 television series "Literary Island". Gordon now lives in his favourite town, Shrewsbury, and enjoys frequent walks in the Shropshire countryside.

Introduction

*I*n the autumn of 1990 I was asked if I would be interested in producing a book illustrating the changing seasons in Shropshire. I did not need to be asked twice - to have a virtually free hand to photograph whatever scene I wanted, and to have the results published, is something which every amateur photographer dreams about.

*S*uch freedom sounds perfect but it does have its problems. Just as freedom generally needs discipline, so photographic freedom requires a structure. If I go out with a camera, just hoping that a picture will appear, I am usually disappointed. I take much better photographs when I set out with a particular location, scene or effect in mind and so, for this project, I tried to set myself a proper brief. Certain locations, features and events were firmly in my mind, some requiring several visits before I achieved the result I wanted. Having over two years to complete the book seemed, at the outset, to be ample time. But as the seasons passed - a rainy spring here, a snowless winter there - I realised that something like five years would be a more realistic time span to do justice to the changing landscape. Picture taking was limited to weekends, occasional spring and summer evenings and part of my annual leave. Needless to say, the best, most photogenic weather always seemed to occur when I was at work or otherwise unable to get out with a camera. A further frustration was the apparent merging of the seasons. We have had several mild winters recently and the other seasons have often not been typical. It has, however, made me more sensitive to the subtleties of the seasons and I hope that at least some of the pictures will reflect this.

I have deliberately not tried to make this a tourist guide to Shropshire - there is no picture of Stokesay Castle, for example, nor of the Iron Bridge or several other accepted tourist locations. And I have not tried to cover equally all corners of the county. Since I was asked to make a personal interpretation of the seasons in Shropshire my own preferences have come through - you will therefore find pictures of the Stiperstones district, of the south Shropshire hills and certain other locations where I feel at home, where the landscape affects me and where, on those rare occasions when all the elements combine, my photograph becomes a sort of emotional response to what I see. There is nothing unusual about this - I am sure we all experience something like it from time to time but not everyone tries to capture it on film. It does explain why some places seem to draw me back time and again in an attempt to capture the mood or atmosphere. There are other parts of the county where I have lingered, places which I knew and loved as a child, for example, although sometimes the present view was less acceptable than the remembered one. And there are places, most notably the meres and mosses of north Shropshire, which I did not know very well, but whose charms have now caught me.

Shropshire Seasons

*A*s I have travelled around the county, sizing it up time and again through the viewfinder, I have begun to ask myself what it is which makes Shropshire so special. This has not been a deliberate process, more a subconscious questioning. It is only as I write this that I realise that the process had even been taking place in my mind. I have not arrived at a definite answer to my question. But perhaps that is the answer in itself - it is the combination of Shropshire's intangibility, its reticence, its constant sense of understatement which is unique. Its hills are not dramatically high, its lakes and meres are not vast, its scenery is modest but it is anything but bland. It is a landscape which whets the appetite, which satisfies but never leaves you sated - only wanting more of the same. It is difficult to put into words but is experienced by many and once experienced few can escape its hold. Why else do so many people come here to live and work, fully intending to move on after a year or so ... and end up staying permanently?

*S*hropshire has a wealth of geological features which explain the variety of its scenery. Its market towns are mostly dotted around the perimeter, looking outwards to Cheshire, Staffordshire, Herefordshire, Powys and Clwyd. So each of these neighbouring counties helps mould that adjacent bit of Shropshire, most obviously through the dialects and accents of its inhabitants. There is no such thing as a Shropshire accent, there are many. And I doubt whether many people outside the county could confidently attribute any of them to Shropshire.

*A*nother factor in Shropshire's intrinsic character must be its position, sharing a border with Wales and, over the centuries, influencing and being influenced by this neighbouring country. Again, this can be heard in local accents, seen in the form of Welsh place-names and revealed in certain customs and traditions - for example the annual eisteddfod at Minsterley. It is interesting to see how the very name of Shropshire has been used by authors, such as Dickens and Austen, to symbolise the countryside, rural isolation. This was developed further by E. M. Forster in *Howard's End* where the fictional Oniton (actually Clun) is seen as the antithesis or even the antidote to commercial London - it begins to take on a symbolic function, the romance of the west where the sun sets over the hills. Housman's "blue remembered hills" have a similar effect. The poet manages to summon up a nostalgic image of a romantic rural past which may never have existed however much we might like to believe in it.

*A*s I write this I find my thoughts on Shropshire proliferating - I could go on but will spare the reader! I hope that you will enjoy the photographs and that you will forgive me for not including your favourite place or view. I hope also that you will take every opportunity to enjoy and cherish what we have on our own doorsteps - a beautiful county which will take a lifetime truly to discover. I feel that I have only just begun.

Gordon Dickins

June 1993

Spring

"*L*oveliest of trees, the cherry now
Is hung with bloom along the bough,
And stands about the woodland ride
Wearing white for Eastertide."

From A Shropshire Lad, A. E. Housman.

Crow's Nest Dingle

*T*his old cottage, exposed to the elements two thirds of the way up the dingle, was always the last sign of habitation before emerging onto the bleak uplands of the Stiperstones. Sadly, the elderly couple who struggled to live on here have now gone - but for one who passed by occasionally, the memory of their steadfast independence remains.

On Earl's Hill

*I*n order to depict the changing seasons in Shropshire I had, before starting on the project, imagined certain scenes and subjects which could not fail to capture the reader's attention. However, I had determined not to include cliched shots of irresistible woolly lambs with protective mothers. But I did say irresistible!

Harley

Bypassed by the main road Harley has now regained its sense of peace and quiet. With its lovely old church, half-timbered cottages and views of the wooded escarpment of Wenlock Edge, it is a delightful village. Frances Pitt, the famous naturalist, writer and photographer, lived here at Castle House from 1958 until her death in 1964.

Caer Caradoc

Caradoc is the highest of the ancient
pre-Cambrian hills (the others being
Ragleth, Helmeth, Hazler and the Lawley)
which stand across the valley to
the east of the Long Mynd.

From Caer Caradoc

Like so many of Shropshire's hills
Caradoc is crowned by an extensive Iron
Age fort, its massive banks and ditches
linking outcrops of rock to form a secure
enclosure - a testimony to the single-
minded industry of our predecessors.

Below Long Mountain

*R*ural mail facilities in deepest Shropshire.

Ashes Hollow, Long Mynd

*T*he vast plateau of the Long Mynd,
formed in the Pre-Cambrian period some
five hundred and seventy million years ago,
is now scored by deep valleys or "batches".
Ashes Hollow is one of the most beautiful
of these, thankfully inaccessible to motor
vehicles and consequently unspoilt.
This view was taken in March with the bright,
rusty brown of dead bracken and fern
being the dominant colour on the hillsides.

Badger

*T*he village was once part of the Badger Estate. Badger Hall, home of the eighteenth century writer Isaac Hawkins Browne, was demolished in the early 1950's. Together with nearby woods and the famous Badger Dingle with its pools, ravines, follies and other delights, the whole area was an extended pleasure ground for the big house. The thatched cottages clustering around Town Pool are as pleasing to the eye today as they must have been to generations of the wealthy from the Hall. Whether life in the cottages was as idyllic, is perhaps less certain.

Primroses at Stanley

Cowslip

Hall Close Coppice, Alveley

Badger Dingle

*B*adger Dingle lies between the villages
of Badger and Stableford and would have been
well known to the young P. G. Wodehouse.
His parents had bought a house in Stableford
and their son, home for school holidays from
Dulwich College, came to know the nearby
villages and countryside. There are many thinly
veiled descriptions or references to them in his
novels and stories. Badger Dingle, for example,
becomes "Badgwick Dingle" in his school
story *The Pot-hunters*.

Cole Mere

*E*arly spring at Cole Mere with the first flush of green in the trees and the water lying still in the clear light.

Cole Mere is one of many lakes or meres in north Shropshire, formed after the Ice Age when post-glacial hollows filled with water.

It is ringed by woodland and a delightful circuit walk offers tantalising glimpses of the water.

The Mere, Ellesmere

*T*he Mere attracts hundreds, if not thousands, of water birds. Some, such as the Canada Geese, are almost tame and populate the mere-side approaching Ellesmere. Others, more elusive, seek the further reaches of the Mere and provide a compelling attraction for the many visiting ornithologists.

Eaton Mascott

"*It was a perfect day*
For sowing; just
As sweet and dry was the ground
As tobacco-dust."

From Sowing by Edward Thomas

Shropshire Union Canal
near Cole Mere

A quiet canal scene in early May,
before the onset of the tourist season.
Down below the embankment, to the right,
are the strangely named Yell Woods.

Coundmoor Brook

*T*aken on one of the rare fine days in the spring of 1991, there is plenty of water in the brook and lush new growth in the verges alongside the little used lane to Acton Pigot.

*B*leached, dead grasses from the previous summer contrast with a fresh carpet of grass, richly studded with celandines.

Aston on Clun, Arbor Day

*T*he black poplar tree in the centre of the village
is, by tradition, always decorated with flags,
a custom originating in 1660 when Charles II
designated a day in May as Arbor or Tree
Dressing Day. Aston on Clun is thought
to be the only village in the country
to maintain the custom.

*T*he blackened faces place the Morris
dancers firmly in the borderland. A tradition
which some facetiously attribute to the local breed
of black-faced sheep, but others claim was
a disguise for the dancers to avoid recognition
when they begged from the crowd.
The "tatter" jackets have evolved from an earlier
tradition of pinning strips of coloured cloth onto
ordinary clothes to create dancing costumes.
Here the "Shropshire Bedlams" perform.

*I*n 1786 a local landowner, John Marston, married Mary Carter.

As the wedding coincided with Arbor Day the villagers of Aston on Clun decided to revive the tree dressing custom.

The Marston family perpetuated it until 1951. Since then it has fluctuated but in 1991 the ceremony was widely publicised

and traditional Morris dancing, a "wedding" procession and a village fete were all part of the programme.

Here local children re-enact the Marston wedding of 1786.

Haughmond Hill

A relatively new crop in Shropshire,
the vivid yellow fields of oilseed rape have now
become an expected part of the scenery in May.
Beyond the field Haughmond Hill offers
attractive walks and fine views
over Shrewsbury.

From Douglas's Leap, Haughmond Hill

Following the Battle of Shrewsbury,
tradition has it that the Earl of Douglas
was captured after falling from a rocky outcrop
on Haughmond Hill, perhaps close to the spot
where this photograph was taken.

Hope

*H*oly Trinity has surely one of the
prettiest locations of any church in Shropshire.
The Hope Valley winds its way up from Minsterley
and the church lies below the road, reached by the
white footbridge crossing the stream which cuts
through the churchyard. The Hope Valley was
used by Mary Webb as the setting for her novel
The House in Dormer Forest.

LightspoutWaterfall, Long Mynd

The valleys, cut by fast-flowing streams, which characterise the eastern edge of the plateau provide some of the finest scenery on the Long Mynd. This waterfall is one of the more spectacular sights but one often missed by thousands of visitors to the Cardingmill Valley who amble up to the point where two streams meet but go no further. Those who turn left and trek a further few hundred yards up Lightspout Hollow are well rewarded.

Linley Hill from The Rock

*A*pril, and the last remnants of a late snowfall persist in the shaded nooks of Linley Hill.

Old Oswestry

*T*his superb example of an Iron Age hillfort, covering over thirty acres, consists of a complete series of earthen banks and ditches. Most of Shropshire's forts, and there are many of them, are sited on the summits of hills. Old Oswestry, although commanding extensive views over the present town and surrounding countryside, lies on gently rising ground - barely a hill. There is easy access to the fort and it is pleasant to walk around the peaceful ramparts, perhaps imagining less peaceful scenes of bygone times.

Offa's Dyke near Selattyn

*T*his great earthwork, its building ordered by the
eighth century Mercian king, Offa, can be seen
clearly here in this stretch to the north-west of
Oswestry. The dyke was presumably some kind of
boundary between Wales and Mercia and ran from
near the present day Prestatyn in the north
to Chepstow in the south. A long distance footpath
now follows its entire length and this is one of the
most beautiful sections, seen against
a backdrop of remote hills.

River Severn near Melverley

*T*aken on a warm, misty, languid May evening
close to the Severn's confluence with the Vyrnwy.

Papermill Bank, River Roden

*T*he Roden winds its way through
the flat countryside of north Shropshire,
between the sandstone outcrops of Hawkstone
and Grinshill, eventually to join
the River Tern at Walcot.

Snailbeach Mine

*R*emains of old winding gear, collapsed in situ, at Snailbeach which, during the last century, was one of the richest lead mines in the country. In march 1895 it was the scene of a terrible accident when seven miners were killed. They were being lowered in the cage down one of the main shafts when the steel cable broke. The accident occurred when they were half way down the two hundred and fifty yard shaft, the helpless victims plummeting to their deaths. Witnesses afterwards claimed that the cage, normally over seven feet high, had been compressed to just eighteen inches by the impact. A whole community went into mourning.

Pontesbury

*A*n impressive line-up of tractors for sale is indicative of the agricultural economy upon which Shropshire is so dependent.

Laura's Tower, Shrewsbury Castle

*P*arts of the castle date from the twelfth century, but Laura's Tower was added in 1790 on the site of the original keep.

It was Thomas Telford who designed it and who transformed the castle into a private residence for Sir William Pulteney who was

MP for Shrewsbury from 1776 to 1805. Pulteney is best known for his association with Bath (Pulteney Bridge).

Laura's Tower celebrates his wife's name just as, in Bath, she is commemorated by Laura Place.

The Abbey Church, Shrewsbury

*T*he Abbey was founded towards the end of the eleventh century, for the Benedictine Order, by Earl Roger de Montgomery. Today the Abbey Church is the only substantial surviving building of the original complex. Many of the monastic buildings were destroyed by Thomas Telford's Holyhead Road - ironic that the engineer we so venerate should have committed such vandalism! Nowadays we associate (or are encouraged to associate, by promoters of tourism) the Abbey with Brother Cadfael, the fictitious medieval sleuth who is achieving world-wide popularity created by Shropshire author Ellis Peters. That intrepid traveller and dry observer, Celia Fiennes, was not over-impressed with the Abbey but she did approve of the Abbey Gardens:

"... with gravell walks set full of all sorts of greens orange and lemmon trees ... out of this went another garden much larger with severall fine grass walks kept exactly cut and roled for Company to walke in; every Wednesday most of the town Ladyes and Gentlemen walk there as in St. James's Park and there are abundance of people of quality lives in Shrewsbury more than in any other town except Nottingham."

From The Journeys of Celia Fiennes 1698

Weston Under Redcastle

*W*eston, a cluster of stone and half-timbered cottages, lies close to Hawkstone Park.
Like Norton it has managed to retain the village stocks, just out of sight here below the churchyard wall.

St. Michael's Church, Madeley

*M*adeley was the first of the once separate townships to be subsumed by Telford New Town in the 1960s.

My thoughts on what the planners did to Madeley are best kept to myself but I take some consolation from the fact that the church and

the area around it remain relatively "unimproved". The place is most often remembered for the ministry of John Fletcher, the man who John

Wesley had in mind to succeed him as leader of the Methodist movement. Fletcher's original church, in which he and Wesley preached

to vast congregations, was demolished, to be replaced by Telford's church of 1796, seen here at the top of the sloping churchyard.

Near Poles Coppice

I could not believe my eyes when I first caught sight of this unfortunate beast with his head firmly stuck in the fork of a tree. After I had run half a mile to summon help from the nearest farm, the farmer arrived, in a mood less sympathetic than my own, and set to with a saw. The animal was duly released, never knowing how close it had come to being decapitated, and trotted off to rejoin his mates.

Shipton

*S*t. James's Church dates from Norman times and its weather-boarded tower and elevated position make a picturesque scene when viewed across the fields in front of Shipton Hall.

Shipton Hall

*T*his lovely old house looks out over the Corve Dale towards Brown Clee. With its mullioned windows, ornate chimneys and mellow limestone walls Shipton Hall could almost have been transplanted from the Cotswolds.

Oss Mere

*O*ne of the most enjoyable things about producing this book has been the opportunity to seek out and visit places previously unknown to me. I do not know north Shropshire as well as the south, so it was a pleasant surprise to discover that the meres extend beyond the Ellesmere district. Oss Mere, near Whitchurch, is a gem - an extensive stretch of water in a beautiful setting and ringed with Alder trees, many of them growing out of the mere itself.

Norton

*T*he stocks and whipping post at Norton have survived in spite of the efforts of errant drivers to mount the kerb and inflict permanent damage on these ancient bits of village history.

Eyton on Severn

*T*his elaborate summer house
(or prayer tower as I have heard it described)
is virtually all that remains of the original
mansion built here by the Newport family
in the early seventeenth century. Eyton was
the birthplace of Edward Herbert, Lord Herbert
of Chirbury. Edward, the elder brother of the
poet George Herbert, was himself a poet,
diplomat, philosopher and historian.

Ragleth Hill

*R*agleth, the most southerly of the Stretton Hills, is seen here from the road between Little Stretton and Minton.

The photograph was taken on one of those days in early March when, though no new growth is to be seen, it nonetheless feels like spring.

Brown Moss

This nature reserve, south-east of Whitchurch, is managed by Shropshire County Council's Countryside Service, who have set out nature trails and produced explanatory leaflets. It is a beautiful but delicate site, a mixture of heathland and woodland with shallow pools interspersed, supporting varied and often rare wild plants. For anyone interested in the subject *Shropshire Meres and Mosses* by Nigel Jones (published by Shropshire Books) is recommended.

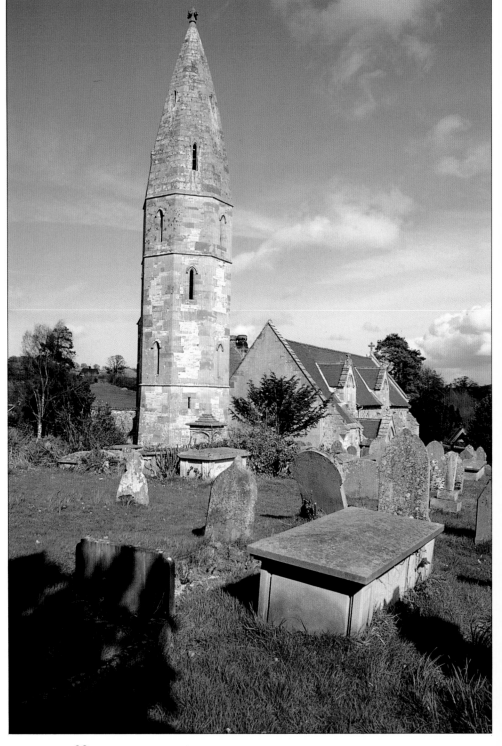

Llanyblodwell

*F*rom its name you would hardly expect still to be in England, but you are - a village on the River Tanat, close to the Welsh border. The church is unique, its tower usually described as cigar-shaped but looking to me more like a rocket about to be launched into space. It was designed by the vicar, the Reverend John Parker, in the middle of the last century and he was responsible also for the extravagant decoration inside the church.

Mountain pansies

*T*hese rare spring flowers were spotted
on a south Shropshire hillside.

Nesscliffe Hill

A sheer sandstone cliff, cut like a piece of cheese,
is evidence of past quarrying on the hill.

The Breiddens

*N*ot one but several hills, straddling the border with Wales and seen here in dramatic light across the Severn Valley.

Summer

Acton Reynald

A warm summer afternoon, an idyllic rural backdrop and twenty-two players give their all to an English ritual - the village cricket match.

Black Marsh Stone Circle

*S*tapeley Hill is well known as the location of Mitchell's Fold stone circle. Less well known is this circle of low lying stones, of similar Bronze Age antiquity, which are to be found in a boggy area below the hill. Unlike Mitchell's Fold this circle has a central stone, seen here in the foreground. In the distance is the ruined engine house of the Ladywell lead mine.

Callow Hollow, Long Mynd

*C*allow Hollow is deep
in shadow and the moon has already
risen on this July evening.

Near Robin Hood's Butts, Long Mynd

*L*ooking towards the Stiperstones. Although similar in height the two upland blocks of the Long Mynd and the Stiperstones are quite different both in structure and in atmosphere. Mary Webb used this powerfully in her first novel, *The Golden Arrow*, giving the two landscapes symbolic powers which work upon the emotions and actions of her characters.

Ashes Hollow, Long Mynd

*T*he setting sun on a clear summer evening illuminates this stunted Hawthorn against the deep shadow of the valley beyond.

Stoke on Tern

*I*am not sure if there is a typical north Shropshire scene but if there is such a thing then this might be a good example -

lush meadows, grazing cattle, a wide sky. Here the big Victorian church is built a little way from the village,

from a distance looking almost like a ship in full sail.

St. Eata's Church, Atcham

*L*ate sunlight catches the red sandstone
of the tower and seems almost to reflect the
warmth of the day. The dedication of the church
to St. Eata is unique, and equally unusual is the
fact that the lower parts of the tower are possibly
Roman in origin, built with stone which may
have come from the ruins of Uriconium,
the Roman city just a mile or so away.

*W*hen planning shots for this book I visualised an idyllic church, deep in the country, with ivy-clad gravestones, rooks overhead and the congregation chatting in small groups around the church porch as the vicar bids them farewell. I therefore lurked about several churchyards, invoking suspicious looks, in pursuit of this photograph. Perhaps I was unlucky in my choice of churches but on each occasion the faithful either dribbled out in ones or twos or galloped out to their Volvos and BMWs and off home, presumably to complement spiritual sustenance with Sunday lunch. But patience was rewarded and after more lurking about in this churchyard at Atcham I got more or less the shot I wanted.

Bomere Pool

*S*ituated midway between Lyth Hill and Condover, Bomere Pool was well known to Mary Webb who frequently walked here and enjoyed the peace and tranquillity of the rippling waters and the sound of the wind in the encircling trees - if she were alive now I am not sure that she would appreciate the roar of motor boats towing water skiers. Bomere was almost certainly the direct stimulus for her fictional "Sarn Mere" in *Precious Bane* although she probably drew upon her knowledge and memories of Cole Mere and Blake Mere, in the north of the county, also.

In her story Sarn is unforgettable, an influence for good and ill on the characters who know it:

*I*t is the story of us all at Sarn, of Mother and Gideon and me, and Jancis (that was so beautiful), and Wizard Beguildy, and the two or three other folk that lived in those parts, that I did set out to tell. There were but a few, and maybe always will be, for there's a discouragement about the place. It may be the water lapping, year in and year out - everywhere you look and listen, water; or the big trees waiting and considering on your right hand and on your left; or the unbreathing quiet of the place ..."

From Precious Bane, Chapter 1

Blue Pool, Telford Town Park

*T*hirty years ago the area now covered by Telford town centre, from Priorslee almost to Dawley, was one of industrial and mining waste. It was characterised by old pit mounds and spoil heaps, "mounts" as we used to call them, overgrown with grass, bramble and birch. In between were other remnants of the industrial past - old kilns and chimneys and the occasional labourer's cottage, linked by one or two pot-hole ridden lanes and a maze of unofficial pathways. Through the middle of all this ran the railway from Coalport to Wellington, now part of the Silkin Way. When passenger traffic ceased in the early 1950's the Midland Red bus which replaced it followed a tortuous route via Madeley and Stirchley village and on into Wellington - but how could a mere bus replace the famous Coalport Dodger?

*T*oday much of this landscape has been incorporated into Telford Town Park. Beyond the more conventional park features it is pleasing to see that Withy Pool, Randlay Pool and Blue Pool have been tidied, preserved and promoted as attractive local features, rich in wildlife, in the heart of the town. While much of the industrial wasteland of the last century has rightly been cleared or developed it would have been sad if all evidence of this landscape had disappeared. The distinctive Stirchley chimney is seen across Blue Pool, a monument to past generations of Shropshire folk who laboured here and a reminder perhaps, if one is needed, that industrial prosperity is a tenuous commodity.

Severn Valley Railway, Bridgnorth

*B*ridgnorth, always a popular weekend retreat for visitors from the West Midlands and elsewhere, is also a compulsive attraction for those who love steam locomotives. On summer afternoons the platforms are packed with families and enthusiasts enjoying a healthy dose of nostalgia - smuts and all. As a former paid-up member of the Ian Allan Locospotters' Club I feel honour bound to record that the locomotive here is BR Standard Class 4 4-6-0, No. 75069, built in 1955 and withdrawn in 1967.

Giant Horsetail

*C*lass K4 2-6-0, No. 3442 "The Great Marquess"
was built specifically to work the romantic West
Highland Line from Glasgow to Fort William and
on to Mallaig. Withdrawn from service in 1962
it worked steam "specials" for some years before
being brought to Bridgnorth in 1972. The chance of
seeing a rare locomotive such as this on the Severn
Valley Line in BR days was virtually nil, the train
spotters of the 1950s and early 60s having
to be content with more mundane ex GWR
and LMS locomotives.

Bridgnorth Castle

*T*he keep, much damaged by Parliamentarians
in 1646, now leans at the crazy angle of fifteen
degrees (compared with the five degrees of the
Leaning Tower of Pisa). The former inner bailey
of the castle is now an attractive park,
and from here there are lovely views
to Low Town and the river.

Hampton Loade

*H*ampton Loade has, for generations, been a popular riverside venue, a good place for a day out. And the Hampton Loade ferry has, for generations, plied to and fro across the Severn, a practical form of transport and an attraction in its own right.

Bromlow Callow

*A*distinctive round-topped hill, crowned with a circle of trees, Bromlow Callow figures in the novel *Gone to Earth*.
This is an evocative place where, if I believed in such things, I might imagine the spirit of Mary Webb to be at rest.

The Devil's Chair

*T*he Devil's Chair, best known of the tors on the bleak ridge of the Stiperstones, has a firm place in folklore. It is reputedly the meeting place, on St. Thomas's Eve, for all the ghosts in Shropshire. In fine weather the ridge has a benign aspect, as here - a marvellous place to walk and enjoy superb views, east to the Long Mynd, west into Wales. But in bad weather the Devil's Chair and its neighbouring crags take on a sinister aspect - dark. threatening, hostile - uncomfortable places to be if you are not suitably clothed and prepared.

Brockton, near Bishop's Castle

I was photographing the stream which runs through the centre of the village when I noticed these geese, straight out of Beatrix Potter, against the background of a semi-derelict farm building. The urge to photograph them was not to be overcome.

Hughley

*T*he events may have changed but some aspects of village life are the same as fifty years ago - and the means of advertising them remain as basic as they used to be.

On Linley Hill

*W*henever I look at this picture
I can feel the oppressive heat of this August
afternoon. Even the sheep did not know
what to do with themselves.

Old Grit Mine

*A*nother of the many abandoned
leadmines in the vicinity of Shelve.
The brilliant yellow of the gorse makes
a striking contrast with the surrounding
greens. On the horizon the crags and tors
of the Stiperstones are bathed
in light and shade.

Near Ratlinghope

A dilapidated bridge crosses a trickling stream - it could be in almost any rural English county
and yet it is typically Shropshire - timeless, discreet, almost secretive.

The Dingle, Shrewsbury

*T*he Dingle, its formal gardens
in glorious technicolour, is arguably
the pride of Shrewsbury.

St Chad's Church, Shrewsbury

*B*uilt by George Steuart in the early 1790s
from local Grinshill stone, the tower of St. Chad's
is seen to full advantage from the Quarry,
Shrewsbury's public park.

Near Wroxeter

*A*n evening view across the Severn
as it meanders towards Ironbridge. In the distance
is the wedge shape of Acton Burnell Hill and further
right the hump back of the Lawley,
first of the Stretton Hills.

Ellesmere

*T*he canal wharf at Ellesmere is always
worth a second look, there is always some activity
or other to watch - such is the attraction of boats
and water, whether they be inland or on the coast.
Vicky Baker, closely supervised by her dog Doodle,
continues the tradition of painting canal ware.
Not only the pieces she completes for sale
but the truly vibrant decoration of the interior
of her boat are a testament to her art.

The Mere, Ellesmere

*P*leasure boats, birds and children -
a mixture which sums up the appeal of this the
largest of the meres.

Fenn's Wood,
Shropshire Union Canal

*T*his section of the canal is famous for its succession of lift bridges. This is right on the border with Wales, the photograph being taken from the Clwyd side.

Ruyton XI Towns

A long, winding red sandstone village, built along the edge of a hill overlooking the River Perry, Ruyton XI Towns has, as its highest point, an unusual combination of Norman church and castle sharing the same site. The village, as it now is in spite of its name, was one of eleven townships which made up the manor.

Buildwas Abbey

Standing on flat land adjacent to the River Severn Buildwas Abbey is only a mile or so from Ironbridge where the river ceases its meandering and, constricted by the valley sides, begins to rush through the gorge. But here, amongst the ruins of the twelfth century Cistercian Abbey there is absolute peace and, as always in such places, a distinct sense of times past.

Near Loppington

*T*he summer months seem to pass so quickly that it is easy not to notice the transition in the fields from green to gold. And then, suddenly, the harvest is in full flight and the whirrings of combines emanate from every other field and the air is full of dust.

Corndon from Pennerley

*T*he distinctive shape of Corndon Hill dominates the skyline west of the Stiperstones. It is actually just in Wales but its presence very much influences this part of Shropshire. At 1,683 feet it is about eighty feet lower than the Stiperstones.

Kynaston's Cave

*R*eputedly the home or hideout of Shropshire's Robin Hood, Humphrey Kynaston, Kynaston's Cave is literally hollowed out of the sandstone cliff on Nesscliffe Hill. Kynaston's name has passed into local folklore with tales of skirmishes with the Sheriff of the county, of his robbing the rich to give to the poor and of his prodigious feats of horsemanship, most notably in leaping across the River Severn at Montford Bridge. He was outlawed in 1491 but received a pardon before his death in 1534.

The Wrekin from Uppington

*F*or many people the Wrekin symbolises Shropshire, the outcry when the authorities removed the wartime flashing beacon from its summit being at least partial proof of this. Although I have lived beneath it in Little Wenlock for a time, I have never had a particular affection for it. I am not sure why this should be - perhaps because it seems too domesticated, or because it flatters to deceive. At just over 1,300 feet it is of no great height and yet from some angles it takes on the profile of a real mountain, something which the nineteenth century illustrators went to work on, making it look like some kind of Mercian Matterhorn.

The Wrekin from Harley

*H*aving committed heresy by admitting to being less than enthusiastic about the Wrekin I should, in fairness, say that there are some lovely spots below it and that the view from the summit is superb.

Ludlow Livestock Market

Shropshire is still predominantly an agricultural
county, typified by the regular livestock markets held
in most of its towns. Although styles of dress have
changed (in some cases just a little!) and modes of
transport may be different, the livestock sales must
look, sound, feel and certainly smell much the same
as years ago. And they still give the impression of
people having a good day out, even though the
business may be deadly serious.

Ironbridge

*I*deliberately chose not to include a picture of the Iron Bridge itself on the grounds that it has been done before, thousands of times over. I offer instead a view of the town itself, clinging to the hillside as it always did, more prettified than it used to be but still essentially itself. But that subversive streak of nostalgia in me, which dominates all logic, still makes me wish that Ironbridge was as it used to be - tatty, crumbling, just about surviving, still unaware of the impending arrival of the great god Heritage.

*T*he arches, viewed across the river from the Wharfage, are those of the old viaduct which carried the Severn Valley Railway. Ironbridge Station has long since been demolished, replaced by a car park. Right up until 1963 when the line was closed to passenger traffic, the station waiting room was still lit by gaslamps, and on many occasions I started my school homework by this flickering light while awaiting the diesel railcar (ex Great Western, 1930s vintage) from Shrewsbury. As always, nature begins to reclaim what humans think they have made permanent and, in this picture, the woods behind the arches and the foliage below seem destined to meet eventually.

Ironbridge Power Station

*A*t school in Coalbrookdale we could see the cooling towers of the "new" power station rising high above the old one, almost to the top of Benthall Edge. Concrete, utilitarian structures they may be but they nonetheless have a certain visual quality which attracts the eye. Perhaps they are just the natural industrial successors to the ironworks which dominated the district in earlier times.

From the Iron Bridge

*T*his was taken from the bridge, looking down river towards Jackfield and Coalport.

At this time of the year, with the trees in full leaf, the narrowness of the gorge is accentuated.

Uriconium

*T*he Roman remains at Uriconium are extensive and have
fascinated not only archaeologists and historians but writers too.
Dickens visited and wrote a long essay on his observations.
The young Wilfred Owen often used to cycle here from his
Shrewsbury home and Housman, ever mindful of the continuum
of time, reflected upon our ancestry in *A Shropshire Lad*.
And Mary Webb also was sensitive
to the evocations of the ruins:

"*V*irocon - Virocon -
Still the ancient name rings on
And brings, in the untrampled wheat,
the tumult of a thousand feet."

From Viroconium

Whixall Moss

Whixall Moss, on the Shropshire-Clwyd border, is an internationally noted area of peat bog supporting a tremendous variety of rare plant and insect life. The mosses were formed, like the meres, at the end of the Ice Age when the resulting hollows filled with water and vegetation. As this rotted over the centuries it formed a thick layer of peat. Peat cutting has been an enduring feature on Whixall Moss but thankfully the threat of large scale commercial cutting has been averted. Whixall Moss remains a delicate and important site.

Brown Moss

*B*rown Moss has survived for centuries because of an innate balance of climate, landscape and land use. But in recent years these pools have occasionally dried up and there are fears that the unique habitat could be endangered.

River Teme, Bromfield

A hot and drowsy late summer afternoon
at Bromfield near Ludlow, the cow edging into
the river to drink apparently as lethargic
as the photographer.

Song at the Beginning of Autumn

*N*ow watch this autumn that arrives

In smells. All looks like summer still;

Colours are quite unchanged, the air

On green and white serenely thrives.

Heavy the trees with growth and full

The fields. Flowers flourish everywhere.

*P*roust who collected time within

A child's cake would understand

The ambiguity of this -

Summer still raging while a thin

Column of smoke stirs from the land

Proving that autumn gropes for us.

*B*ut every season is a kind

Of rich nostalgia. We give names -

Autumn and summer, winter, spring -

As though to unfasten from the mind

Our moods and give them outward forms.

We want the certain, solid thing.

*B*ut I am carried back against

My will into a childhood where

Autumn is bonfires, marbles, smoke;

I lean against my window fenced

From evocations in the air.

When I said autumn, autumn broke.

Elizabeth Jennings

Autumn

Near Shrawardine

*A*n evening scene of tranquillity in early autumn.

From Haughmond Hill

*T*here are lovely views from Haughmond Hill,
one of the young Wilfred Owen's favourite
destinations for cycle rides during his teenage years
in Shrewsbury. I climbed the hill on this occasion,
laden with camera equipment and tripod, having
parked my car by the Abbey, and soon became
absorbed in photographing the sunset and its subtly
changing afterglow. I was so carried away with this
that I failed to notice that it was nearly dark, and
without a torch I had to make a rather awkward
and stumbling descent of the hill as a result.

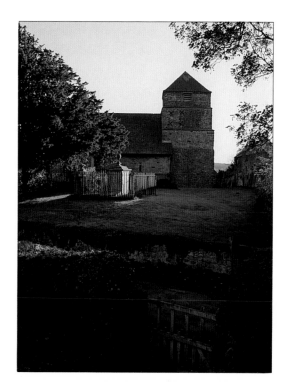

Barrow

*T*he ancient church of St. Giles, dating from Saxon times, stands within the Willey Estate. Simply yet solidly built it still retains much of its Saxon and early Norman stonework.

Near Berrington

I noticed this strange phenomenon, a "rainbow" in the stubble, one morning in early autumn when the ground was strewn with spiders' webs which, in turn, were covered with dew. The bright sunlight completed the prismatic effect.

Apley Park

*T*his Gothic style house, built in 1811 from Grinshill stone, stands above the River Severn upstream from Bridgnorth. Although its castellated battlements and towers are something of a sham it is nonetheless attractive for all that. While it is unlikely to be the actual house which P. G. Wodehouse had in mind for his fictitious Blandings Castle, it conveys the right air and I could almost imagine Lord Emsworth striding the heights of his ancestral pile.

Apley Forge

*A*pley Forge is a little known and secluded
hamlet on the opposite side of the river from
Apley Park - a gem of a spot with a pretty
suspension bridge, white painted cottages
and thickly wooded river banks on either side.
The Severn Valley Railway used to run along
the valley here behind the cottage and there
was even a small station, Linley Halt,
the midway stop between
Coalport and Bridgnorth.

Acton Scott Historic Working Farm

*T*his is not a gipsy's but a shepherd's caravan, presumably used most at lambing time, and similar to the one in which we first meet Gabriel Oak in Hardy's novel *Far from the Madding Crowd*.

*T*he steam threshing machine is a regular visitor to Acton Scott each autumn, a big attraction for visitors. Although, to the modern eye, it might appear to be a bit of a Heath Robinson contraption, its effect and influence in its time should not be underestimated. It was one of the inventions which began to transform farming in the latter part of the nineteenth century. Seeing it in action brings to mind the vivid and disturbing passages in Thomas Hardy's *Tess of the D'Urbervilles* in which Tess is made to work, unremittingly, up on top of the machine:

*"C*lose under the eaves of the stack,
and as yet barely visible, was the red
tyrant that the women had come to serve -
a timber-framed contraption, with straps
and wheels appertaining - the threshing
machine which, whilst it was going,
kept up a despotic demand upon the
endurance of their muscles and nerves."

From Tess of the D'Urbervilles, Chapter 47

Black Rhadley

*W*hile the Stiperstones are well known and much visited the hills immediately to the south west are much more secluded. In the winter months it is often possible to walk for miles around here without meeting anyone.

Below Linley Hill

A rare and perfect autumn day with
bright sunlight enhancing the golds and browns
of the leaves - all too often we miss the autumn
tints because of dull or wet weather during
the precious few days when the decaying
foliage has reached this stage.

Bromlow Callow

*A*lthough Bromlow Callow appears elsewhere in the book I have included it here by virtue of the dramatic light and the unusually clear view of the Breiddens near Welshpool.

Caer Caradoc

*W*hile we might like to think of autumn as the season of rich, golden colours and warm, mellow air, the reality is all too often rather different. Autumn on this particular day was the season of cold, dank fog when a soggy scramble up Caradoc was enjoyable for the exercise but not much else besides.

Corbet Wood

*S*unlight filters through decaying leaves
and the air is warm and heavy with the smell
of autumn in this lovely area of woodland
below Grinshill.

On Linley Hill

*T*his magnificent avenue of beech trees,
unfortunately suffering repeated damage in the
gales of the last few years, is one of Shropshire's
outstanding features, a delight to the eye
at any time of the year.

Towards Ragleth Hill

*T*aken from the Long Mynd, below is the road from Church Stretton to Little Stretton and immediately beyond the houses lies the mound of Brockhurst Castle. It was built of stone in the twelfth century, abandoned by the middle of the thirteenth century and today only ditches and banks remain. Behind the castle site the main railway line and the A49 road follow the valley down to Craven Arms.

Mitchell's Fold

*T*here are many Bronze Age circles in Britain finer than this but few can rival its position. It stands on Stapeley Hill, west of the Stiperstones, with marvellous views over Long Mountain and into Wales. Only fourteen stones remain but the circle can clearly be made out.We cannot but wonder why the people who constructed these monuments, the true purpose of which still remains a mystery to us, chose such bleak and inhospitable sites.

*A*lmost without exception stone circles, burial chambers and other archaeological sites have become embedded in local folklore. Mitchell's Fold was supposedly named after the witch who lived in the locality. Up on Stapeley Hill was a magical cow, miraculously sent to save the population during a famine by providing a constant supply of milk. The only proviso was that just one pail-full at a time should be taken by each person. The witch, deviously, tried to milk her into a riddle - the milk instantly dried up and the cow wandered off to Warwickshire ... and into another legend! Meanwhile Mitchell had been turned to stone and, to ensure that she stayed there, the locals placed a circle of stones around her. The fact that there is no central stone in this circle is just a minor flaw in the story's credibility but we should not quibble over folk tales.

All Saints' Church, Shelve

*T*his simple little church, some eleven hundred feet above sea level, together with a farm or two and a handful of cottages, makes up the village of Shelve, the heart of the old lead mining district. It is a glorious spot with the jagged outcrops of the Devil's Chair and its neighbouring tors capping the heather and bilberry covered slopes of the Stiperstones.

The Stiperstones from Shelve

*I*mmediately ahead, on the skyline, is the Devil's Chair and beneath it scattered cottages - once the homes of lead miners and smallholders. Both would have laboured to eke out a living from this beautiful but inhospitable landscape.

93

Willey

*O*ld farm buildings
and stables, remains of Willey Old Hall,
in the quietest, most secluded
countryside near Broseley.

The Wrekin

*T*his picture was taken in early October on a day which had started overcast
without a break in the cloud. But by mid-afternoon a transformation had taken place and
I was able to photograph the Severn near Bridgnorth in beautifully clear light. As I drove
back to Shrewsbury the light became more dramatic with brilliant, almost metallic sunlight
contrasting with ominously grey banks of cloud. I was near to Cressage so diverted from
the main road, crossed the bridge and managed to snatch a couple of shots of the Wrekin
across the fields of stubble before the light disappeared.

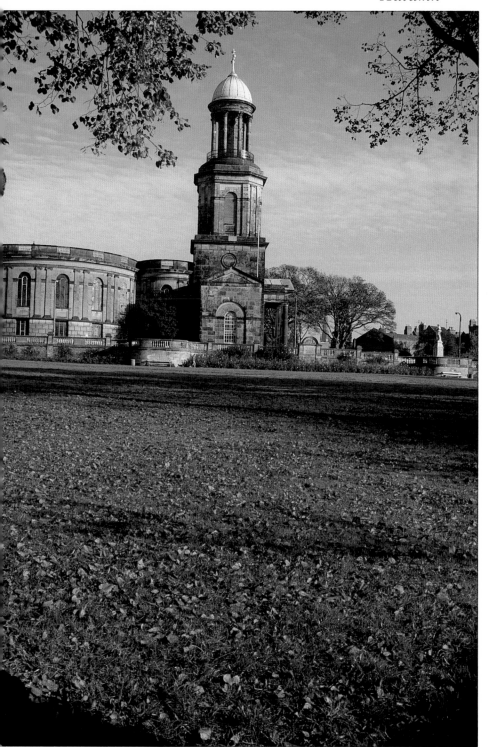

The Quarry, Shrewsbury

*S*hrewsbury is fortunate in having this beautiful area of parkland, some twenty-five acres, alongside the River Severn. Originally a quarry, it was first laid out as a park in the early eighteenth century and has been enjoyed by local people and visitors ever since. Its focal point is the Dingle and the site as a whole is used for the famous annual Shrewsbury Flower Show.

St. Chad's Church, Shrewsbury

A scene in late October of St. Chad's with a foreground carpet of fallen leaves.

*T*hese old type straw bales are becoming comparatively rare sights nowadays as the giant swiss roll variety takes over.

Silver Birch

Little Ness

*J*ust north of the village stands this motte or castle mound, dating back to the eleventh or twelfth century and typical of many to be found throughout Shropshire. Why do some places seem to be fated, as far as the weather is concerned, when I set out to photograph them? Little Ness was a typical example - unremitting, flat grey light always descended the minute I arrived there. Eventually I managed to take my photograph, but even then it totally clouded over within a few minutes. I should not complain .. the bad photographer always blames the light!

Clive

*T*he spire of Clive Church is a well known landmark, visible for miles around. The village, with most of its houses built of Grinshill stone, is most attractive and distinctively north Shropshire in style. The Restoration dramatist William Wycherley was born in Clive in 1640. The writer of numerous plays such as *The Country Wife* and *The Gentleman Dancing Master* he was much more at home in London than in Shropshire, returning only occasionally ... usually to escape his gambling debts!

Melverley

St. Peter's at Melverley is another of Shropshire's gems, a delightful, rustic, half-timbered church, totally unpretentious in design, which dates back to the fifteenth or sixteenth century. The church stands just above the River Vyrnwy, near to its confluence with the Severn and has suffered badly from flooding and erosion in recent years.

River Severn near Buildwas

*T*he Severn, viewed here from Sheinton, meanders gently through its flood plain before entering the Ironbridge Gorge. Just visible on the hill in the distance is the village of Little Wenlock.

Coalport China Works

*T*he name of Coalport was, and is, synonymous with fine porcelain. From 1795, when John Rose and Edward Blakeway went into partnership, until 1926, this factory produced a continuous output of exquisite pieces and patterns. In 1926, following a decline in fortunes, the firm was sold to the Cauldon Pottery Company in the Potteries. The name of Coalport has survived as part of the Wedgwood Group, with many prestigious pieces being produced. And today the old works at Coalport form part of the Ironbridge Gorge Museum, receiving thousands of visitors each year.

Coalport Bridge

*T*he bridge was built in 1818 at Preen's Eddy, replacing a wooden structure which was continually damaged by flooding. Its humpback shape and graceful ironwork continue the tradition of the original cast iron bridge two miles upstream. My childhood home was in Coalport, within sight of the bridge, and I was always in awe of the river - with good reason too, for when it was in full flood, the brown surging waters reached an incredible height, well up the arch of the bridge. In those days the decorative ironwork had rusted away leaving large gaps in some places.

This must have made a big impression on me because I had a recurrent nightmare in which I saw myself, unable to get to my feet, rolling towards one of the gaps and struggling to stop myself falling into the water below!

*I*n spite of the nightmare my memories of Coalport are happy ones. But the place saddens me now. It seems to be a village devoted only to tourism, to Heritage, a worthy attempt to conserve and explain the past. While the historically valuable has been marvellously preserved, other corners of the village are neglected. Could Coalport perhaps be symptomatic of a whole country? And yet, as I commit these thoughts to print I realise that the whole thing is a paradox - I criticise the present for exploiting the memory of the past and yet take refuge in nostalgia myself!

Morville Hall

*T*he Hall and church at Morville present
a picture postcard scene for anyone travelling
along the main Bridgnorth to Much Wenlock road.
This is one of two service wings of the Hall,
eyecatching with its deep red splash of colour
from the parasitic Japanese Ivy.

Brookshill, near Shelve

*T*he leaves have all fallen but there is still bright
colour in the landscape in the form of a prolific
crop of Hawthorn berries.

The Wrekin from Sheinton

*T*he writer and traveller Celia Fiennes visited Shropshire in 1698 and, after stopping in Shrewsbury, set off again for Worcester. She had this to say about what is arguably the county's best known hill:

"... and soe I rode by the great hill called the Reeke (Wrekin) noted for the highest piece of ground in England - but it must only be by those that only live in the heart of the kingdom and about London, for there are much higher hills in the north and west ... this hill stands just by it self a round hill and does raise its head much above the hills neare it ..."

From The Journeys of Celia Fiennes

The Bog

*S*eptember, and the annual show of Rowan
berries is at its best, in this case surrounding
one of the old mine reservoirs. Once there was
a thriving community of mineworkers here with
a school, cottages, a public house and extensive
mine buildings of course. Now most of the latter
have been demolished and cleared,
the school is a field centre and the
pub is a private house.

On Lyth Hill

*L*yth Hill and Spring Coppice just beyond it were Mary Webb's favourite haunts and it is easy to understand why.

The beauty of the hill is matched only by that of the views which it commands in all directions.

105

Titterstone Clee from Nordy Bank

*T*he distinctive scarp shape of Titterstone Clee looms in the distance, topped by the masts and domes of the aviation early warning system which dominate the much quarried summit. In the foreground is one of the great earthen ramparts of Nordy Bank, an iron Age hillfort. Sheena Porter achieved great success and popularity in the 1960s for a series of children's novels set in Shropshire and the Welsh borders. In 1964 she won the Library Association's Carnegie Medal, for the best children's book of the year, for *Nordy Bank* which is set on and around this ancient site. Sheena Porter's stories celebrate the Shropshire countryside and are well worth seeking out, by adults as well as children, for their evocative descriptive passages.

Near Little Stretton

A late autumn skyline, at the bottom of Ashes Hollow,
as the day draws to a close.

Hedgerow

*C*rab apples and Old Man's Beard
are the visible clues to the season,
quite apart from the unmistakable
smell of autumn.

Porthill Bridge, Shrewsbury

Porthill Bridge is one of the most attractive bridges
crossing the river in Shrewsbury, a delicate looking
suspension bridge for pedestrian use only.
Next to it is the well known
Boat House Inn.

Horn of Plenty

Old Rectory Wood, Church Stretton

Sixteen acres of mixed woodland
and another seven of grass make up this site
which is now maintained by Shropshire County
Council's Countryside Service. The path through
the wood leads out, via Townbrook Hollow,
onto the slopes of the Long Mynd.

River Severn near Coalport

A typical view of the Severn along the stretch between Coalport and Bridgnorth where the dense deciduous woods grow right down to the river banks. In this view, looking up river towards Coalport, the leaves have already begun to turn yellow and gold and there has obviously been recent heavy rain if the muddy colour of the water is anything to go by.

Shelve Pool

*F*rom the hill behind Shelve Pool there is a wonderful view of the Stiperstones. This was the landscape which so inspired Mary Webb and was to form the setting for much of her first novel *The Golden Arrow*.

Winter

Atcham Bridge

*T*he old road bridge, with its seven arches, was built by John Gwynne between 1769 and 1771. Through the nearest arch you can just glimpse the "new" bridge of 1929 which, until the Shrewsbury by-pass was completed last year, carried the burden of A5 traffic to and from North Wales.

Atcham

*T*he afterglow of a sunset is often more rewarding to photograph than the sunset itself with subtle, almost luminous colours and no likelihood of flare on the lens. This was taken from Atcham Bridge at the very end of a freezing cold day - so cold that it hurt the fingers to set up and adjust the tripod. Indeed, I was tempted not to bother with the tripod but since, only two days earlier, I had made a New Year's resolution to use one on every possible occasion, my conscience made me persevere!

Acton Burnell Castle

Completed in 1286 for Robert Burnell, Bishop of Bath and Wells, this is really a fortified house rather than a castle, built of bright red sandstone. Beyond, in the adjacent field, stand the two gable ends of what was once a long, low building known as the Parliament barn. The story goes that Edward I, on a visit to Robert Burnell, held his parliament here on this very spot.

Attingham Hall

Attingham always catches the eye as you drive down the old A5 past Atcham. Arguably the finest house in Shropshire, it was designed by George Steuart for Lord Berwick and built between 1783 and 1785. The flood waters in the foreground are those of the River Tern whose confluence with the Severn is only a matter of yards away.

Church of St. Mary Magdalene, Battlefield

*T*he church stands in near isolation on the site of the Battle of Shrewsbury, that bloody conflict between the forces of King Henry IV and those of the rebels led by the Percys, in particular Sir Henry Percy (Hotspur). Many of the facts relating to the battle have been lost but what is known is that many hundreds, if not thousands, of men were killed on the fateful day of 21st July 1403 including Hotspur himself.

*O*ur image of the Battle of Shrewsbury is probably moulded by Shakespeare's King Henry IV Part I, for the battle forms the climax of the play. Shakespeare weaves historical fact with his own inimitable fiction (not least in the substantial but imaginary form of the character Falstaff) to create a memorable drama.

*T*oday Battlefield Church, with its restored nineteenth century roof, displays the coats of arms of some of the knights who fought there. During building work in the last century a large number of bones were discovered, thought to be the remains of some of those killed, their bodies thrown into a pit close to where they fell.

*A*s at many such places the past seeps into the imagination and, at dusk especially, you almost think that you can hear, down the centuries, the receding sounds of battle.

Badger Dingle

*T*he Dingle, landscaped with romantic follies, ruins and pools in the late eighteenth century as a pleasure ground for the Brownes of Badger Hall, is an enchanting place in bright sunny weather. But on sombre, murky days such as this it assumes a claustrophobic air and the passer-by may prefer not to recall the story of Dick Dulson who, disappointed in love, drowned in this very pool late one night ... and whose ghost is said to haunt this part of the woods to this day!

A Shot Magpie

Though on your long-tailed flight
You wore half-mourning of staid black and white.
So little did the thought of death
Enter your thievish head,
You never knew what choked your breath
When in a day turned night
You fell with feather heavier than lead.

Andrew Young

Berrington

A weak, setting sun casts its tint on a scene which could almost have been evoked by Thomas Hardy:

"*W*e stood by a pond that winter day.

And the sun was white as though chidden of God,

And a few leaves lay on the starving sod;

- they had fallen from an ash and were gray."

From Neutral Tones

Brockton

*B*rockton, near Bishop's Castle,
is one of several villages in Shropshire of this
name. The stream which runs through the village
is reminiscent almost of a Cotswold scene.
Shropshire villages, by and large, do not have
the chocolate box prettiness of their Cotswold
counterparts. But they are no less attractive
in their own way, unpretentious expressions
of the working landscapes
to which they belong.

Brown Clee

*B*rown Clee dominates the skyline as you travel towards Bridgnorth from Much Wenlock. Its massive bulk was once topped by an Iron Age hillfort but most of it has been obliterated by years of quarrying. This rather sombre view was taken on a murky afternoon of yellowy light. The white lines in the foreground are the last remnants of snow in the hedgerows following the thaw.

Bury Ditches

*T*his impressive hillfort near Clun used
to be densely covered with trees. The Forestry
Commission eventually cleared them, just leaving
the weird, twisted stumps, to reveal not only the
archaeological features of the fort but one
of the finest viewpoints in Shropshire.

The Flockmaster's Signpost, Long Mynd

*T*his solitary signpost, high up on the Long Mynd, marks an upland junction of ways. The descents to Church Stretton and to Asterton are precipitous and, in weather like this, not for the faint hearted. It was an earlier version of this signpost which Mary Webb described in *The Golden Arrow* - a symbol of safety, stability and shelter.

Cantlop Bridge

*N*ow in the care of Shropshire County Council's Countryside Service, Cantlop Bridge is the only surviving example in the country of one of Telford's cast iron arch highway bridges.

The Long Mynd

*T*housands of walkers enjoy the open expanses of this most popular upland area in Shropshire in spring, summer and autumn.

Not quite so many experience it in bleak winter weather like this when the batches and hollows take on a new and different kind of beauty.

Clun Castle

*C*lun's spectacular castle ruins still dominate the valley and the town, as they have done since Norman times. Sir Walter Scott was a visitor here, reputedly staying at The Buffalo Inn while working on a novel, *The Betrothed*. In it he described a castle, his "Garde Doleureuse", which was probably based on these ruins. A later literary visitor was E. M. Forster who, in *Howard's End*, called the place "Oniton" and wrote evocatively of the castle and its "river girt peninsula".

By the River Clun

I was driving from Clun towards Craven Arms when I noticed this scene which was transformed by the last rays of the setting sun just catching the trees by the house. I only had time to take one frame before the sun disappeared below Steppleknoll.

Corbet Wood

*T*he wood stands on the slopes of Grinshill,
a prominent sandstone ridge to the north-east
of Shrewsbury, and is carefully managed by the
Countryside Service. Hidden amongst the trees are
remains of old quarries; quarries which provided
stone for many of the finest buildings in and around
Shrewsbury, such as the old Shrewsbury School
at Castle Gates (now the Town Library).

Near Habberley

*O*n this cold, grey February afternoon the forlorn expressions of the cattle were understandable. One equally cold and forlorn photographer had every sympathy with them!

Harnage

*M*uck spreading is hardly the most romantic of subjects but it is a typical winter activity on the farm. The dazzling sunlight following a bone hard frost certainly caught the eye.

The Devil's Chair, Stiperstones

An exposed dome of moorland and scattered rock, the Stiperstones have their own special atmosphere. The brooding presence of the Devil's Chair has for centuries generated stories and superstitions which have been used by folklorists and writers alike. The Chair is the dominant symbol of negation and despair in Mary Webb's novel *The Golden Arrow*, a physical presence which undermines emotions and highlights human fallibility:

"So the throne stood - black, massive, untenanted, yet with a well worn air. It had the look of a chair from which the occupant has just risen, to which he will shortly return. It was understood that only when vacant could the throne be seen.
Whenever rain or driving sleet made a grey shechinah there people said, "There's harm brewing." "He's in his chair." Not that they talked of it much; they simply felt it, as sheep feel the coming of snow."

From The Golden Arrow, Chapter 4.

*W*hile Mary Webb knew this place intimately,
D. H. Lawrence would have had just a fleeting view following
a short visit to Shropshire to see his friend Frederick Carter in
Pontesbury. Yet he too chose to use the Devil's Chair
symbolically in his short novel *St. Mawr* and hinted at the same
echoes of evil from this primaeval outcrop of rock:

"*T*hey came at last, trotting in file along a narrow
track between heather, along the saddle of a hill,
to where the knot of pale granite suddenly cropped
out. It was one of those places where the spirit of
aboriginal England still lingers, the old, savage
England, whose last blood flows still in a few
Englishmen, Welshmen, Cornishmen."

From St. Mawr, D. H. Lawrence

High Vinnals, Mortimer Forest

*T*here are tremendous views into Herefordshire
from this point, close to the Forestry Commission
look-out tower. An already beautiful landscape
is further enhanced by the covering of snow
and the orange-pink light of the setting sun.

Mortimer Forest

*T*he end of a bitterly cold day on the Shropshire-Herefordshire border - a fiery setting sun and sheep waiting expectantly, thinking that I would bring them food.

Holdgate

*T*he traditional red telephone boxes are fast
disappearing, some of them to become expensive
decorations in certain suburban gardens.
I decided to capture this one for posterity in its
native surroundings in the Corve Dale.

Lee Hill

I thought I knew Shropshire pretty well but had never visited Lee Hill previously. It is reached from Lee Brockhurst and offers marvellous views from the top. The effort of walking up there was repaid, not only by the view over north Shropshire and back to the Wrekin, but by the beauty of the slender birches amidst the burnished colours of dead fern and bracken.

River Severn near Leighton

*T*his view, from the top of Leighton Bank
is a perennial favourite. The combination of snow,
flood and brilliant light created, briefly,
a magical scene.

Mucklewick Hill, near Shelve

A little ingenuity has turned this defunct farm waggon into a serviceable fence and gatepost.

Moreton Corbet

*T*his attractive group of buildings can be glimpsed from the grounds of Moreton Corbet Castle. The Norman church of St. Bartholomew, extended and restored over the centuries, contains many memorials to the Corbet family. Outside, just visible in the photograph, is a bronze statue of Mercury by J. H. M. Furse in memory of Vincent Corbet who died in 1903 at the age of thirteen.

Near Booley, north Shropshire

I had passed by this pool several times without every considering
it worth photographing. But on this occasion it was transformed by the cold,
clear changing light which picked out the trees leaving the hills beyond,
towards Hawkstone, in deep shadow.

Moreton Corbet Castle

*T*he ruins of the manor house,
begun by Sir Andrew Corbet and continued
by his son Robert, stand adjacent to the
original Norman castle. Robert died in 1586
before the hall was completed and today the
shell of this elegant building is a romantic
legacy of Elizabethan times.

Near Newcastle on Clun

A typical Clun Forest scene, looking west from Offa's Dyke over steeply sloping hills which rise to twelve hundred feet or so. It is an isolated area with just the occasional hamlet or solitary stone farm house. A glance at the Ordnance Survey map will reveal the strong Welsh influence here, most obviously through the place names - Bryn-mawr, Duffryn, Cwm Ffrydd.

On Offa's Dyke

A tired and weatherbeaten line of trees straggles uphill, like a column of exhausted walkers, along the dyke towards Mainstone.

Earl's Hill

A misty sunset over the Stiperstones. Down below, hidden by the curve of the hill but obscured anyway by the mist, is the village of Habberley.

Near The Bog

A traditional green lane, edged by
Hawthorn and Blackthorn trees, the latter
providing an excellent crop of sloes in the autumn.
Sloe gin can be thoroughly recommended ...
in moderation!

*R*ecipe:

9/10 oz. fresh, ripe sloes
4/5 oz. white sugar
1 bottle gin

*S*talk and wash the sloes.
Dry them and slit each one.
Dissolve the sugar in the gin and pour over the sloes
(best not to use all the sugar at first -
sweeten according to taste)
Pour into a jar, seal it and store in the dark
to retain the deep colour.
Leave for about three months, shaking occasionally.
Strain the sloe gin through a fine sieve.
Bottle and serve as a delicious liqueur.

Wenlock Edge

*T*his is one of the classic views from the Edge near Presthope, looking south-west towards the Stretton Hills. Wenlock Edge is a dramatic limestone escarpment running for four or five miles south-west from Much Wenlock and immortalised by A. E. Housman in *A Shropshire Lad*

Harnage

Shropshire Libraries' mobile library service bring literature to those parts of the county which other libraries cannot reach. Not only does the mobile bring books, information and access to other services, but the opportunity for a fortnightly social gathering.

Near Cound

*T*hick hoar frost has persisted
throughout the day, the sun not having
sufficient warmth to melt it.

Marchamley Hill

*L*ate afternoon sunshine filters
through the trees along this lane which is
close to the extravagantly landscaped
grounds of Hawkstone.

Below Earl's Hill

*W*hy as children do we always assume
that tree trunks are brown in colour? They are
actually just about every colour but brown,
particularly in the winter when mosses and fungi
thrive in the wet conditions. Clear, bright winter
days are often the most satisfying for photography,
the natural colours and tones in the landscape
being enhanced by the quality and direction
of the light rather than flattened
by the summer sun.

River Severn near
Belvidere Bridge, Shrewsbury

*T*his was taken just a matter of yards

from my home during the big freeze of 1982

when parts of the Severn actually froze.

Longdon-upon-Tern

*T*homas Telford left his mark upon Shropshire in many ways. Here, in 1794, he built the world's first cast iron aqueduct to carry the Shropshire Union Canal over the River Tern.

Allscott

During the autumn and winter months a continual stream of lorries and tractors converges on the sugar beet factory at Allscott.

The sweet smell emanating from the factory throughout the day and night can often be detected miles away.

This is an important industry in such an agricultural county.

Mytton's Beach, Stiperstones

A view down Mytton's Beach to Stiperstones village. The snow which had fallen several days before now had a thick crust of ice which was difficult to walk on. I had reached this spot via Crow's Nest Dingle, a walk which would normally take about fifty minutes. This time it took two hours and although it was freezing cold I was decidely hot and bothered by the time I got to the top. Several times I fell through the ice crust into deep snow drifts ... but the view was worth the effort.

Lawley and Caradoc

A dramtic sunset over the Stretton Hills. The silhouetted building in the middle distance is Frodesley Lodge,

a grey, stone Elizabethan house which may originally have been a hunting lodge.

Hoar Frost

*T*hick hoar frost temporarily fossilises the grasses, surrounded by a sea of ice.

Much Wenlock Priory

*T*he extensive ruins of this once
great Cluniac priory acquire further gilding
in the form of a thick covering of snow which
seeks out nooks and crannies in the stone
to give highlight and emphasis where
previously there was none.

*M*ore books on Shropshire published by Shropshire Books:

Shropshire From The Air

Michael Watson and Chris Musson   £13.99

Shropshire Meres and Mosses

Nigel Jones   £ 4.99

For a complete list of Shropshire Books titles please contact:

Shropshire Books

Shropshire County Council,

Leisure Services Department,

Winston Churchill Building,

Radbrook Centre,

Radbrook Road,

SHREWSBURY SY3 9BJ.

Telephone: (0743) 254043